Readymades

Readymades

AMERICAN ROADSIDE ARTIFACTS

Photographs by Jeff Brouws

Introduction by Diana Gaston

Essays by Jeff Brouws, Wendy Burton, Bruce Caron, Mark Frauenfelder, Joel Jensen,
M. Mark, Phil Patton, Alan Rapp, Luc Sante, and D. J. Waldie

CHRONICLE BOOKS
SAN FRANCISCO

Library of Congress Cataloging-in-Publication
Data available.

ISBN 0-8118-3677-0

Manufactured in China

Designed by Jeff Brouws and Wendy Burton Brouws,
For A Small Fee, Inc.

Distributed in Canada by Raincoast Books
9050 Shaughnessy Street
Vancouver, BC V6P 6E5

10 9 8 7 6 5 4 3 2 1

Chronicle Books LLC
85 Second Street
San Francisco, California 94105

www.chroniclebooks.com

for Wendy, my delight and illumination

Table of Contents

Introduction
Places in Between

Diana Gaston

"The secret of photography is, the camera takes on the character and personality of the handler. The mind works on the machine."
—*Walker Evans*

JEFF BROUWS'S PHOTOGRAPHS are often compared to the 1930s documentary work of the Farm Security Administration (FSA) photographers, as his images explore many of the same vernacular themes. The comparison has a certain logic. Brouws's ongoing photographic survey seeks out the quiet American dramas within humble structures, amusement parks, small towns, and back roads with a similar reverence. And yet his contemporary vantage point is decidedly different, looking back across the intervening decades and making note of its future ruins. His images reveal a compulsion for storytelling, framing distressed equipment and worn signage as a kind of shorthand for family disaster, economic downturn, and ill-conceived business plans. These photographs find him peeling away the slick finish of urban development to reveal a longer stretch of history and a less self-conscious version of America underneath.

The images presented here fall into neatly prescribed typologies: abandoned trailers, drive-in theaters, partially painted pickup trucks, signs, empty boxcars, and abandoned gasoline stations, among others. Isolated from their original environment and reframed as distinct objects, Brouws's subjects are imbued with a kind of startling dignity they might not otherwise hold on their own. These peculiar finds are regarded as readymades in and of themselves; and his pictures recast these inert objects with an ironic significance. The subjects provide an index to vernacular culture, a means of cataloging anonymous lives and embedded messages. Brouws's production of the past few decades reveals different strategies for getting at the most penetrating material—some subjects are chanced upon during long road trips, others are staked out with great attention and focus—but throughout the various bodies of work is a fervent desire to consume and collect, to assemble a more complex view of American culture than any one of us might hope to know on our own. His images catalog a vast landscape of industry, abandonment, loss, and fortitude, sifting through what we cast off as our most enduring and revealing history.

Brouws's method of collecting certain subjects began quite early, before he even picked up a camera. As a kid growing up in Daly City, a suburb just south of San Francisco, he collected baseball cards, stamps, and endless strings of facts about U.S. history. He soon discovered an amusement park within driving—or hitchhiking—distance from his home, and for a summer he thumbed his way there at every opportunity. The sheer spectacle of the midway,

tucked in against the Pacific Ocean, represented all the exuberance and eccentricity that was sorely lacking in his tidy suburban neighborhood, and he was captivated by the possibilities he found there. Later, in 1987, when he began seriously photographing the genre, his own boyhood amusement park had been demolished, and he began the process of seeking out carnival midways in other cities. The method of deliberately searching out subjects probably began here, a roving photographer scanning the landscape for bits of ephemera, and seeing intrinsic value in them.

For many contemporary photographers, Walker Evans's documentary work of the 1930s and 1940s continues to exert a profound influence. Not so much in terms of subject matter—although Evans photographed the American scene with a remarkably contemporary eye—but rather in his clarity and unembellished directness. As

the critic Andy Grundberg observes of Evans, "he photographed precisely what others had purged from their pictures: telephone poles and wires, road signs, passing cars, a broom leaning against the cardboard wall of a shanty. He saw in these things the rudiments of a uniquely American language. . . ."[1] Brouws, too, acknowledging an affinity for Evans's photographic sensibility, defines American life through its vernacular subjects. He reads the signs that are given, picturing without inflection what they reveal about a particular time and place. This sensibility leads him to photograph subjects that are vaguely similar—of businesses run into the ground or barely holding on, of absurd and brazen signage, of snatches of life in small, inconsequential towns. Brouws photographs the quotidian details that are particularly telling of contemporary culture. His images contain a wry humor, but also a fondness for the unabashed attempts at survival that he finds in these remote places, their mean beauty shaped by necessity.

Brouws frequently mentions the significance of TOADS in his work, what cultural anthropologists refer to as "temporary, obsolete, abandoned, or derelict sites." For him, there is a need to photograph these sites before they collapse, or disappear altogether. It takes some effort to maintain a sense of his photographs' actual place in history, so readily do his subjects slip back in time. The humble gasoline stations that Brouws photographed hold the same poignancy to our contemporary eye as a Walker Evans general store or an Edward Hopper late-night diner. Particularly when he shifts from color to black-and-white, Brouws's photographs have a tendency to isolate the subject as a weary icon from an earlier time. The photographs themselves hover in an uneasy space, existing as both a contemporary document and a touchstone to another era. Even so, a clapboard structure photographed in the 1930s and a very similar structure photographed in the 1990s are, in actuality, completely different structures. The subjects might be similar, even similarly regarded by the photographers, but the times in which the photographs are made create distinctly different social and political contexts, and therefore different readings. As Thomas Southall succinctly expressed in his discussion of Walker Evans's and William Christenberry's parallel explorations of Hale County, Alabama, "Their photographs of similar subjects automatically have different connotations when viewed in the age of Reagan and Bush rather than Roosevelt."[2] The same is true of Brouws's work, which follows a similar documentary vein as his predecessors; the global conditions that shape our contemporary economy and politics are quite different from the conditions in which the 1930s photographer or painter made their imagery. A defunct business pictured in the Depression era holds certain associations for a contemporary viewer—frequently nostalgia for a simpler time—while a defunct business in the year 2003 incites a different set of responses, probably edged with anxiety about current economic conditions. Brouws explores this space in between, in which the history and dilapidated state of his subjects trigger a complex reading. His images salvage cultural ruins not to dwell in their particular time and place or to inappropriately borrow from the nostalgia of the period, but to acknowledge their passing. His images memorialize the stuff that is discarded or abandoned. The photographic documentation at once eulogizes their mundane past and posits them as significant historical markers.

Brouws's photographic approach presents an expansive inventory of common structures, describing worn surfaces and peculiar details with gracious attention. While his work on the American highway and carnivals has consistently displayed a penchant for deep resonant color, he has simultaneously been at work on images that are much more spare in their treatment. His recent cataloging of abandoned gasoline stations, drive-in theaters, and grounded travel trailers reflects a more literal, less dramatic interpretation of his subjects. In their cool, straight-on reading in black-and-white, his images pay homage to Ed Ruscha's self-published artist books of the 1960s, such as *Twentysix Gasoline Stations* and *Every Building on the Sunset Strip*. In these images Brouws is deliberately stripping away the transcendent color and light of his earlier work to present the subject in the most factual terms possible. Like Ruscha, who photographed gasoline stations along the drive from his home in Los Angeles to Oklahoma City, Brouws

renders many of the same stations with equally deadpan, objective description—something approaching a Sears catalog of structures encountered on the road. In Brouws's hands, however, a narrative element insinuates itself into his pictures, pervading even the most desolate subject with a larger story. The images faintly glow with their own fiction.

Taking on such iconic subject matter as the American highway and the development of the West is difficult. It is well-traveled territory, with a long history of photographers stretching from Walker Evans, Wright Morris, and Edward Weston in the first half of the twentieth century to Robert Frank, Robert Adams, Lewis Baltz, Lee Friedlander, and Joel Sternfeld in the latter half. Brouws navigates this territory knowingly, occasionally striking familiar chords with earlier imagery, but always with a very clear sense of his own personal document. In his late-night

photographs of remote gasoline stations, for instance, his melancholy structures draw an easy comparison with Robert Adams's image *Frontier Gas Station and Pikes Peak, Colorado Springs, Colorado,* made some thirty years earlier. Like Adams, Brouws frames the immensity of the Western landscape in a square format, utilizing the most economic of aesthetic means to describe the harsh glow of fluorescent lights against the outline of the mountains beyond. For both photographers, working in different places and from different perspectives, the gasoline station signifies much of the same longing and disappointment offered by the mythical stretch of Western highway. Adams witnessed its domestication, commercialization, and overcrowding, and thirty years later Brouws sets up his camera in front of an abandoned gasoline station to pay tribute to the end of its run.

Brouws's work generally reflects a

11

practiced documentary stance, one that keenly observes a particular subject within the space of its surrounding environment. But he doesn't always operate from a safe or neutral distance. In the series of travel trailers he enters into a fairly intimate space with strangers, pushing his camera up against their neglected property. He photographs the once sleek and promising vehicles in their most pathetic state, propped up on blocks, crammed full of junk, immobile, and utterly beaten. Through his repetition of this particular subject, photographed in black-and-white, dead center, and from the same uncomfortable proximity, a distinctive pattern emerges; one that inventories the various states of the vehicle's demise from private space, to second bedroom, to padlocked storage shed, to family defeat. For anyone of Brouws's generation, the travel trailer represents a short-lived attempt at European design, technical innovation, and

family mobility. Travel trailers, first introduced to consumers in the 1950s, encapsulated the American desire to travel, to roam, to have all the conveniences of home on the open road.[3] To see them rendered useless, deteriorating under harsh light and neglect, brings a fairly sobering realization about our cultural ambitions, and how quickly they are overturned and replaced.

In searching out abandoned gasoline stations, abandoned drive-ins, and bowling alleys across America, Brouws operates under the assumption that he might easily find one of each in nearly every small town he comes across. There is comfort in the realization that so many American towns are laid out with such predictable order. Main streets are flanked by two-story buildings, with storefront windows on the first level and private offices and apartments above; government buildings, schools, and banks are close to the cen-

ter of town; recreational facilities—bowling alleys, drive-ins, and baseball fields—are generally located on the outskirts. Gasoline stations parallel the highways, and are sited a bit farther out of town. There is a prescribed order, a logic, to the layout of small-town America, not unlike the order found in Brouws's own photographic typologies. Landscape historian J. B. Jackson argues that this trend towards uniformity, now so prevalent in suburban developments and shopping centers, actually reaches back throughout our history. The modern development, in its conformity and tidy layouts, reveals "an authentic, latter-day expression of the classical American style: simple, easily understood, and not without elegance . . . [They] have always proliferated in the United States; Plymouth in the seventeenth century was such a one; the frontier outpost, the railroad town, the company town were others. We produce them by instinct."[4] Given this penchant for conformity, it is all the more remarkable to discover small outbursts of eccentricity along the edges. These rough spots serve to act as our cultural subconscious, the soul-saving stretches where order and neighborhood associations all but dissolve.[5]

The repetition that Brouws deliberately seeks out, sometimes chasing a single theme across thousands of miles, results not only in a photographic collection of subjects, but a document of individualism stretching from region to region. It is not impossible, his images remind us, to find a novel approach to living even as the tradition of modern American development moves us steadfastly towards conformity. He collects subjects that at once reflect this instinctual tendency toward classical, predictable uniformity, but also reveal some element of individualism. He delights in the eccentric personalities that blurt out absurd messages on hand-painted signs,

or erect a twenty-foot-high bowling pin against the Mid-western sky to advertise a bowling alley. In his fragmentation of commercial signage he creates his own quirky messages, as if to release the most pertinent information from the larger text. He also finds it in the wild color combinations of partially painted pickup trucks, the random patterns signaling the possibilities of a work in progress. Through his exhaustive search across the country for such imagery, he discovers a quiet defiance against conformity in the most unlikely of places. It is here, in these remote towns, in the places in between, that small businesses and unique building solutions have the best chance of surviving. Not for long, of course. And this is what gives a certain urgency to his work, to document even the slightest trace of individualism, as expressed through vernacular architecture, signage, run-down vehicles, and main streets. Here, among

the ruins and outskirts of American life, he locates the best version of us.

NOTES

1. Andy Grundberg, "Walker Evans, Connoisseur of the Commonplace," *Crisis of the Real* (New York: Aperture, 1990), p. 68.

2. Thomas W. Southall, *Of Time and Place: Walker Evans and William Christenberry* (San Francisco: Friends of Photography and Fort Worth: Amon Carter Museum, 1990), p. 29.

3. See J. B. Jackson, "The Moveable Dwelling and How It Came to America," in *Discovering the Vernacular Landscape* (New Haven and London: Yale University Press, 1984), pp. 91–101.

4. J. B. Jackson, "The Love of Horizontal Spaces," *Discovering the Vernacular Landscape*, p. 69.

5. See Rebecca Solnit, "After the Ruins," in *Art Issues,* November/December 2001, pp. 18–22.

1

FRESHLY PAINTED HOUSES

Ticky Tacky

Jeff Brouws

I DON'T BELIEVE THERE is an "average American," but it was a term adopted by the media, one I remember from my youth. Memories come back to me of the relaxed intonation of Walter Cronkite's voice coming over the evening news on CBS. It possessed a sermon-like quality and finality. His nightly closing "and that's the way it was," offered reassurance. Each evening as we faced the television set, secure in its maple cabinet that my father had built, we heard facts that were never questioned. Statistics were emerging about daily American life then; about what the average American thought, felt, believed. If Walter told us something it was surely the truth. He controlled the facts of our lives. We were immersed in, and yet protected by, our innocence. The media and Cronkite wouldn't lie to us, would they?

I never questioned my "averageness." Of course I was average. I lived in a housing tract where all the homes stood in a stifling, controlled symmetry. Variation was not welcomed. The same house with the same front lawn and floor plan stood across the street. All the fathers slowly backed their late model Fords or Chevys from their garages each morning at the same time and went to work. All the mothers stayed home and all the kids went to the school down the block. Our collective "averageness" was a front, a shield to hide the hidden discrepancies, our separate secrets.

Bobby James's mom and dad were raging alcoholics who never raised their blinds, went to work, or mowed their yard. It retained a brown, shabby deadness year-round, reflecting the turmoil within. A turmoil unwitnessed, but suggested. Bobby had a glass eye that he would remove from its socket upon request: the neighborhood freak. I never asked how it got that way and he never volunteered to tell me. Those days weren't as confessional. It was late 1963, President Kennedy's assassination a stain across the country's consciousness. The media and the government did keep the truth from us as we kept personal truths from each other. We sequestered our individual problems and neuroses. For instance, we all knew that Bobby James's parents routinely beat the shit out of him (and each other), the beatings the possible explanation for his disability, but we didn't discuss it. Nor the pain behind our own walls. Yet it was the one thing that made every family on the block unique, the unspeakable pain hidden by the commonality of the trimmed and tightly mowed lawns, or the close-cropped military haircuts our fathers all wore.

It seemed as though my parents were the first to divorce on Mayfield Avenue. I was seven at the time and, for the first years of my life, remember only seeing my father in the evenings and on Sundays.

The rest of the time he worked or was in the garage hitting golf balls against a large, immovable piece of canvas he had stretched across the width of the space. Standing at the kitchen door I could look down the stairs and watch the small white orbs collect on the concrete. I sometimes retrieved them with a little red canvas "shag bag" that hung from a hook above his workbench. I enjoyed watching his swing. It was this nightly metronome-like sound of the club head against the ball, that still recalls the place for me. This sound is my father. Precise, even-handed. Eventually, he left, leaving my mother and me in the house. He later remarried and returned to the neighborhood. I had moved away by then, to live in an apartment building on Eastmoor Avenue. I was the first, but definitely not the last, kid on the block to witness the break up of our families.

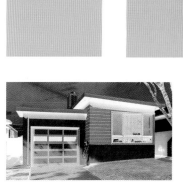

FRESHLY PAINTED HOUSES 1991

Sea Foam
11B-9U

Mint Leaf
12A-56D

AFTER MANY YEARS PASSED I came back to the neighborhood to visit my father and stepmother and noticed that the houses surrounding theirs had been painted in vibrant splashes of color. Driving through this housing tract that had first been built by Henry Doelger in the mid- to late '50s, to provide shelter and a piece of the American Dream to returning Korean War veterans, I began noticing many homes on other blocks painted in similarly bright hues.

At the time my father and stepmother had decided that Daly City was becoming too crowded. Or so they said. In actuality, this being the late '70s, fear of minorities or "the Other" moving into what had been predominantly white neighborhoods, was burgeoning. Of late, there had been a tremendous influx of various ethnic groups of Filipino, Chinese, and Korean descent buying their first homes in the neighborhood (and in America), so they

too could begin their climb up the economic ladder. The earlier generation of home buyers (my parents) in the area saw this influx as an opportunity to take their profit and cash in, move to a "safer" place, buying something closer to the "country" and farther out from the urbanized "edge." Real estate values had tripled in twenty years. It was time to move on. The "white flight" had begun.

NATURALLY, EVERY CULTURE has different aesthetic sensibilities, one of these being sense of color. This is very evident if an American travels to some place as close by as Mexico or as far away as Manila; the buildings are oftentimes painted in vibrant tones of yellow, orange, green, or turquoise. Colors that usually don't show up in a housing tract in America. It is also true that in many little seaside villages in Greece (where all the buildings are white to reflect away the intense Mediter-

ranean sunshine), each household, in an act of individualizing their home, paints the flower boxes in the front yard or the stones on the front walk in unique, bright colors. Well, the same thing was happening in Daly City. Asian immigrants, in remembrance of their culture and homeland, were also individualizing their cookie-cutter, little-boxes-on-the-hillside homes, by painting trim and body in

colors no middle-class, mainstream American would dare display. It was cool and in direct contradiction to many of the gated communities, condominium complexes, or zoning ordinances rising up across the land—ones that demanded that all units be painted in "officially sanctioned" earth tones or similarly drab colors, the colors themselves suggestive of the unimaginative architecture that is so indicative of America's present suburban housing stock. I find it both ironic and delightful that in one of this country's first suburban tracts—Daly City, California, known for its stifling sameness—a unique, human trait prevails.

Lilac
12A-45A

Dingo
13A-45A

Seashell   36D-5E

Carmen Red   57B-2T

Tango Blue 77B-3D

Hyacinth 73C-2A

Blue Slate   10A-2E   Pepto Pink   49B-2C

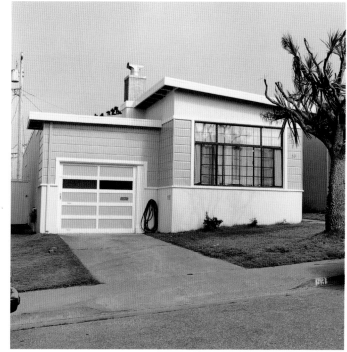

23

Oceana   45D-7A

Slightly Salmon   47B-4C

Cohoe   33D-6B   Tapioca   15E-7B

25

Brownie   28A-7C

Flamingo Fever   54F-2C

Pretty-in-Pink 16F-5D

Coral Surprise   27T-2C

Mandarin   57D-2F

Ramona   24A-5E

Green Boy   60B-4D

Icy Cool   57D-9B

Hint-o-mint   60B-1P

Sherbert 30D-1A

Tawny Taffy 35B-7C

Charcoal   18A-4F

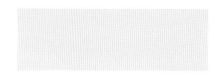

Lemon Zest   24A-3C

MAN

For

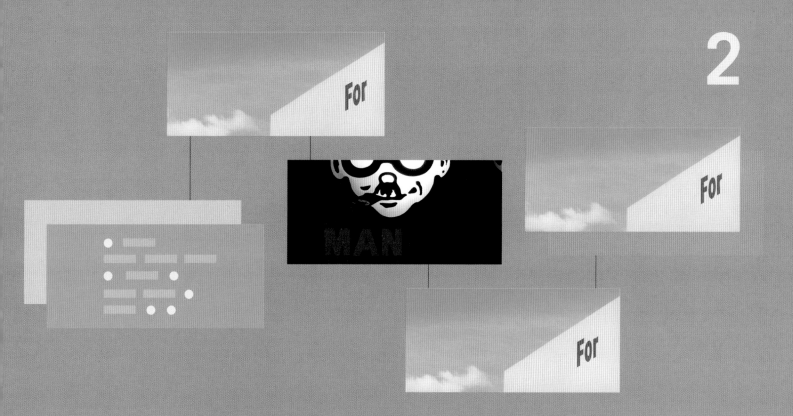

2

LANGUAGE IN THE LANDSCAPE

The Emancipated Word

D. J. Waldie

WOOZY WITH THE WORDS pouring out of a text-intoxicated English culture—which had already produced Shakespeare, the King James Bible, the popular ballad sheet, and the scurrilous broadside—Americans in the eighteenth century knew that language embodied salvation. How else except by the Word were unruly human hearts to be broken and contentious citizens reformed to make a New Jerusalem? The book and the landscape lay open before Americans: God's word held in a grid of his book's orderly columns and the wilderness howling outside.

Thomas Jefferson thought that the making of America on the "blank sheet" of the continent was an act of rational composition, but only for the literate. For Jefferson, to read was to be free and the notion of a literate slave an impossibility. Jefferson presumed that his field hands would always be illiterate—the ultimate definition of a non-participant

in the American story—but archeology at Monticello hints that some of Jefferson's slaves subverted this racist ideal and schooled their children in the citizen's skill of reading.

Jefferson understood (and feared) that literacy was not a neutral tool but one with a protean capacity for transformation. He knew, after all, reading's erotic attraction. He imagined a national text penetrating forests, fording rivers, and passing across prairies behind pioneers like Lewis and Clark, leaving a grid of townships and sections that would extend uniformly from the Alleghenies to the Pacific Ocean. But he was anxious, in a peculiarly American way, about the passage of that narrative into the hands of any huckster, charlatan, or snake oil salesman with a signboard.

In bibliolatrous America, where encounters with the printed word still set men and women trembling in the nineteenth century to build or buy newer utopias, it was too late to constrain the promiscuous play of democratic language in the landscape, that public spectacle of the emancipated word.

WHEN I WAS A BOY in the 1950s in California, when to drive seemed limited only by the various edges of the continent, the transfixing boredom of a long family trip was abated, at some point in the afternoon of the first day, by one of us reading aloud the passing billboards to no one in particular. In the West, long stretches of summer-brown high desert were subdivided by billboards counting down to an attraction that was 25 . . . 15 . . . 10 . . . 5 . . . 2 miles away until THIS IS IT! in letters thirty feet high hung over the reptile farm/date orchard/Indian relics/coldest beer/mystery spot by the side of the road. The billboards advertising them were ugly, intrusive, shrill, and still comforting as signs from a realm outside.

My brother or I, reading billboards aloud, proclaimed that forward progress was being made, that something settled would eventually punctuate the emptiness,

and that staying was an option even when the arrow-straight highway, clinging to a map line approved by President Jefferson, said to go on.

Reading billboards, if only briefly, overcame the silence that inevitably collected in our family car. Mingled in their sales pitches was as much yearning as an appeal to buy. In the impermanent country of the highway, the language of billboards pleaded for a relationship—if only over a counter for a bottle of soda—more nakedly than anywhere else. Every sign was hung on a scaffold of hope.

IN OLDER CITIES, SOME PAINTED SIGNS (often those facing north, because they are less faded by the sun) offer products and services hardly even imagined anymore: MILLINERY, FIREPROOF HOTEL, CLOTHES IN THE NEW YORK MANNER, SYRUP OF FIGS, TRUSSES, ARTIFICIAL LEGS, TAXIDERMIST SUPPLIES.

These signs, some still asserting brand loyalty after a hundred years and some a palimpsest of competing sales pitches bleeding through successive decades, are more than a museum of past desires or a record of fashions in advertising (and least of all merely nostalgic). Old signs are part of a dialogue that is continually shaping American places, in the same way every neighborhood that unexpectedly survives its own era overcomes the national pastime for the new and our easy habit of forgetting. America bristles

with public conversations that aren't about you and me and that were begun without our presence and will continue after. Language on walls remembers, even when our preference is amnesia.

Preserved public speech traces and retraces memory in the air above our heads. There is a connection between its tenuous survival and our own. The disposability

IMMEDIATE MARRIAGE / Victorville, California 1990

FEATURING HIGH PRESSURE / Dover, North Carolina 1990

WE HAVE / Victorville, California 1990

QUALITY PARTS / Cheney, Washington 1992

USEABLE MATERIALS / Chicago, Illinois 2001

REPAIR / Cleveland, Ohio 1999   **BEN YELLEN** (for Ed Gregory) / Brawley, California 1989

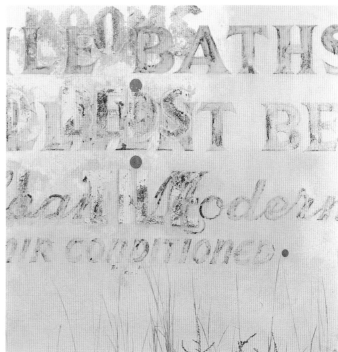

A LOT TO GIVE / Ernul, North Carolina 1990   **CONDITIONED** / Allamore, Texas 1996

TRY / Santa Rosa, New Mexico 2000

FOR / Lancaster, California 1995

YES / Steubenville, Ohio 2001   **NO** / Taft, California 1987

TEMPERANCE / Atwater, California 1991

BEARINGS / Butte, Montana 1999

OPTIC / Las Vegas, New Mexico 1993

MONEY / Denver, Colorado 1995

ONE SQUEEZE PROVES / Bend, Oregon 1987   **TERRIBLE** / Banning, California 1991

MAN / Bakersfield, California 1991

POP ME / Holbrook, Arizona 1992

SOME PEOPLE WILL SAY ANYTHING / Olancha, California 1991

OUR GREATEST THRILL / Bethany, Oklahoma 1993

WELL CLEANED, WELL PRESSED / Redwood City, California 1988

LET US HELP YOU / Lodi, California 1991

DANGER / Formosa, California 1992   **1 MILE, ONE PERSON** / Mojave, California 1993

STANDARD / Schuyler, Nebraska 1999

RUSCHA / Lula, Oklahoma 2001

3

ABANDONED DRIVE-INS

Enormous Bodies in the Night

Luc Sante

DRIVE-IN MOVIES WERE IN their heyday when I was a child, but I was only fleetingly aware of them. My parents and I were immigrants from a country that had no drive-ins, where the very notion would have been preposterous, and my mother in addition was piously terrified of them. The infection of the world by immoral movie images was bad enough, but drive-ins polluted the open air. Only once or twice a summer did I catch glimpses of enormous bodies in the night, when we drove back from the Jersey shore and, on a viaduct near Perth Amboy, hove within range of a screen. Once, though, as we were backing out of a parking space at a chain store on a highway strip, the entire windshield was suddenly filled with the image of Samson, standing between two plaster pillars, pushing out with his arms as rubble fell from above. I saw the screen for all of fifteen seconds, maybe, before my mother ordered me to look away, but the effect was as shattering as if I had been there in the temple. The image lived in my dreams for months, maybe years. As it happens, I didn't attend a drive-in until the summer after high school. The earth had revolved on its axis a few times by then; the picture was *Last Tango in Paris*. My mother may have saved me from the cavortings of Frankie and Annette, but that apparently only made me all the more eager to see Marlon Brando sodomizing Maria Schneider.

That was in 1972, when the drive-in phenomenon was in full decline. Families with children were no longer the principal customers, so smut entered the arena, and the playgrounds were yanked from their berth between the screen and the first row of cars. The drive-in has enjoyed a parabolic career. The first theater, where movies were projected from the top of a car onto a bedsheet, opened in Camden, New Jersey, in 1933. By the end of the Second World War there were about a hundred nationwide; three years later, over eight hundred; a decade after that, nearly five thousand. Drive-ins were built that could hold thousands of cars, where shuttle trains ferried customers to the concession stand during intermission, where rock bands played and bathing-suit contestants paraded on a platform before the feature, that advertised themselves with triumphal entrance monuments out of Babylon by way of Nuremberg. When the most hubristic of the theaters started adding bad-weather enclosures with seats, decadence had set in. But television was the main culprit for decline, which began in the mid-1960s; every decade thereafter saw the drive-in census drop by a thousand or so. Now there are again

about eight hundred in the land, and none at all in New Jersey.

It is estimated, however, that something like a thousand dead drive-ins decorate assorted patches of real estate between the oceans. They were built by people innocent of the past and hungry for the future, who probably expected their constructions to be, one day soon, superseded by something much more titanic. That is to say, they weren't meant to last. They were made of plywood and aluminum, basically, and with half the care and savvy required by a chicken coop, and so they look much more ancient than their years. Their former audiences may harbor nostalgic vignettes— of necking with some long-ago paramour while fourteen-foot insects took over the world on the oblong in front of them— but at the same time consider that the history of the moving picture began with the latest gizmo to fill a corner of their recreation room. The survival of dead

drive-ins only proves that there remain parcels of open land that have not yet been sectioned up into housing developments.

But then again you can find yourself driving on some two-digit state road out in the purple sage, hypnotized by the red sun that sits an inch above the horizon directly ahead, thrown further into an odd frame of mind by the radio station that has unaccountably chosen this moment to resurrect Roy Orbison's "Devil Doll," and then you come upon one of these remnants—a sail-shaped sign with letters down its spine that spell Mesa or Luxor, a board with a scatter of black plastic letters that spell nothing, a huge rectangle with missing slats, maybe a collection of what look like parking meters sprinkled across a furrowed field. At such a moment the drive-in becomes a mute witness to a bygone civilization, as lonely as a fallen column and as saturated as a Greco-Roman amphitheater. And that is the aura that photographs of dead drive-ins succeed in conjuring: Each of those screens is a stele, or a menhir, and we know nothing about their builders other than that they were giants, with overwhelming confidence in their rule over the landscape. They were wiped out by invaders, or disease, or a meteor. They had to be, or how else to explain their neglect of their sacred spaces?

N° 51 / Uvalde, Texas 1996   N° 41 / Lenwood, California 1994

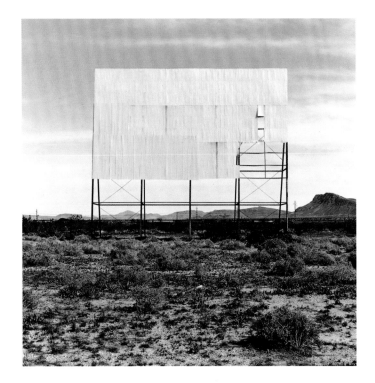

N° **77** / Parker, Arizona 1995   N° **33** / Mississippi 1995

N° 84 / Lovell, Wyoming 1999

N° 23 / Chinook, Montana 1999

N° 68 / Sheridan, Wyoming 1999   N° 6 / Fresno, California 1992

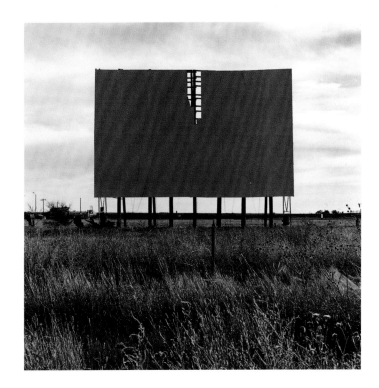

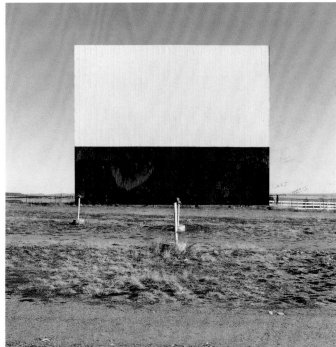

N° 26 / Liberal, Kansas 1993   **N° 72** / Las Vegas, New Mexico 1993

N° 9 / Anacortes, Washington 1994

N° 14 / Tyndall, South Dakota 1993

N° **10** / Litchfield, Minnesota 1993   N° **31** / Schuyler, Nebraska 1993

N° **3** / Lompoc, California 1992   N° **1** / Santa Barbara, California 1992

N° 55 / La Mesa, Texas 1998   N° 30 / Alleghany, New York 1998

73

N° 66 / Ada, Missouri 1993

N° 27 / Bridgeport, Nebraska 1999

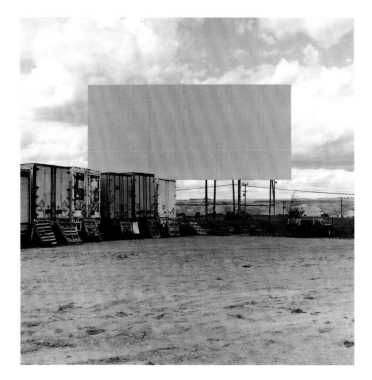

N° 90 / Shelby, Montana 1999

N° 21 / Kansas City, Missouri 1995

N° 60 / Montana 1999   **N° 99** / Utah 1992

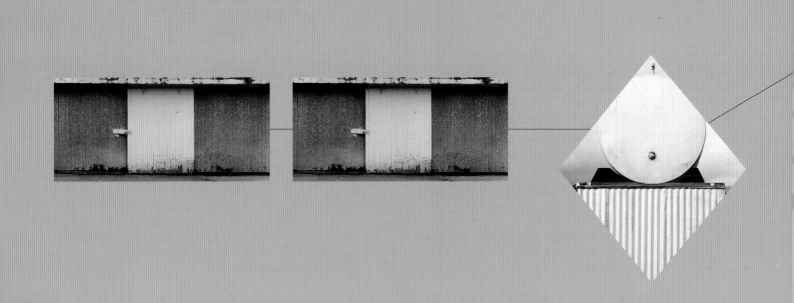

4

FARM FORMS

Heartland

M. Mark

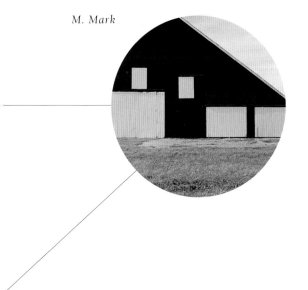

HERE IN NEW YORK, when the subject of hometowns arises, I can usually count on staking my claim to exoticism. "Waterloo, Iowa," I say, with a certain amount of pride. "Home to both the National Dairy Cattle Congress and the mighty green and yellow John Deere tractor. Heart of the heart of the country." My companions tend to gaze at me with curiosity, as if I've just said "Outer Mongolia" or "Mars." Last month, however, at a very civilized party given by the president of Vassar College, my impeccably urbane dinner partner, a classics professor, made Waterloo sound ordinary. "I was born in Moose Jaw, Saskatchewan," he announced, and then softened the blow by relating an anecdote: Thirty-five years ago, soon after he'd come east for graduate school, he and his classmates were invited to tea at the dean's house. Upon learning that one of these classmates hailed from Iowa, the dean's wife remarked, "How extraordinary. In this part of the world, we pronounce it 'Ohio,' you know."

Sad to say, despite spending my first sixteen years in Iowa, despite being the only child of a man who worked for thirty years—worked with dedication and unflagging loyalty—in the business office of the John Deere Waterloo Tractor Plant, I am in some ways almost as ignorant as the dean's wife about America's heartland, or at least the traditional American vision of what that heartland is and ought to be. The Waterloo–Cedar Falls metropolitan area has a population of 128,000, a university, a symphony orchestra, well-stocked public libraries, excellent public schools. My childhood was standard-issue suburban: ballet and tennis lessons, neatly trimmed lawns, shrubs sculpted into shapes not found in nature. My knowledge of farms came from glimpses of gently rolling hills and distant buildings clustered among trees, fleeting green-gold long shots through the car window while we were headed someplace else. Years later, in New York's Hudson Valley, I was finally ready for my close-up of life on a family farm.

In the spring of 1986, worn out after the death of my mother, the last of my close kin, I needed a break from the rigors of Manhattan, where I'd lived for a decade. A friend who had a weekend place on a dairy farm in Dutchess County, ninety miles north of the city, told me about an empty nineteenth-century tenant-farmer's house down the lane. "It looks like grandma's gingerbread cottage," he said. "How bad could it be inside?" The kitchen, it turned out, was done up in avocado: color-coordinated stove, refrigerator, and linoleum. Acoustical tile on the ceilings, Holiday Inn oatmeal carpet on the floors, Reel-Wud paneling on the walls (the logo appeared, with a flourish, every few

feet). But the windows were large and relatively clean, and the landscape outside the windows looked like paradise: hills that reminded me of northeastern Iowa, horses and cows scattered amid greens so intense and tender that the world of the farm resembled a huge, delicious salad. We rented the house, and every weekend that summer I sat on the back porch, soaking up consolation. The trees that separated our yard from the pasture—slender, elegant locusts a hundred feet tall—seemed particularly precious to me, particularly reminiscent of the Iowa countryside.

A freak snowstorm hit the Hudson Valley in early October, while the leaves were still on the trees. I awoke before dawn to what sounded like gunshots and, as the sun rose, watched the weight of the snow split my beautiful locusts. They fractured, one by one; they cracked like

breaking bones. Late that afternoon, Henry Wheeler, the man who had farmed this land for the better part of fifty years, stopped to help us shovel our car out of a snowdrift. After listening to me mourn the trees, Henry said with characteristic mildness, "Oh, well, in seventy or eighty years, you'll hardly see the difference." That was the first of many lessons I've learned from Henry: Those trees weren't planted for my viewing pleasure; nature has its rhythms; there's not much room for sentimentality in the life of a farm. Henry is a Quaker, a conservationist, a retired schoolteacher, a wise and modest man, a bit of a romantic, a bit of a scamp. Six years ago, he gave Peter and me a memorable gift. The day before our wedding, Henry arrived, tall and gaunt and grinning, on the front porch. "Brought your present," he said, and pointed across the road to the hill where he'd mowed two fifty-foot hearts. "It's crop art," he explained. Peter and I got married in a great big heart; during the ceremony Henry read from Emerson's essay on friendship.

There's a sense of community on the farm that has something to do with the land. Hills tuck into each other, enfolding neighbors' houses, keeping us together even when we go for weeks without seeing anything more intimate than lights in the distance on a winter's night. In summer, greenery blocks visual contact, but the connection remains strong. The house on the highest hill belongs to the Angell family: mother, father, eight children, each with a biblical name and crucial job in the hen house or paddock or milking room. The Angell farm crew has gradually taken over much of the day-to-day work as Henry settles into his eighties. (Yes, Angells watch over us. Reality, as we all know, often encompasses the improbable.) I spend about half of each week in the country, writing and teaching, and until a couple of years ago, my life had a pleasing symmetry: I thought I had returned to a landscape very much like the one in which I was born.

Then David Lynch gave me a shock. *The Straight Story* is a very slow road movie, a tender-hearted quest tale about penance and forgiveness based on the journey of a real-life Iowan. In 1994, Alvin Straight learned that his brother in Wisconsin, from whom he'd long been estranged, had had a stroke. Alvin was seventy-three, and his eyes weren't good enough for him to drive a car, so he rode three hundred miles on his John Deere lawn tractor. Lynch shot the movie in 1998, shot it in sequence, in real time, following the route Alvin had taken, fifty miles north of my hometown, clear across Iowa to the Mississippi River and beyond. Alvin passed several handsome farm buildings— passed them at 5 mph—and took shelter in a shed so voluptuously weathered that the walls seemed to consist primarily of sky. Halfway through the movie, I fell through a hole in time. After decades back East, I suddenly saw what Thoreau called "the fabulous landscape of my infant dreams," and it was not at all the landscape of New York. The difference was partly a matter of scale: Hills in Iowa seem to isolate buildings, spread them out below the enormous sky. Partly it was a matter of light, which changes perceptibly when the ocean is half a continent away. I had a good long cry. Like Alvin Straight, Lynch is not afraid to take his time, look hard, let silence accumulate as he gets to know what's in front of his eyes. Like Henry Wheeler, he appreciates buildings and people when they're useful and allowed to show their age.

Yesterday, nearing the end of this essay, I decided to take a slow walk around our farm. Out the front door, across the road, the field that once had hearts mowed in hay is now striped with curving rows of corn. Down the dirt lane, on the right, the locusts stand tall and narrow in lopsided splendor. Farther along, on the left, are the farm's gray-shingle manor house and the weathered red milking barn, its tin roof artfully streaked with rust, its outbuildings shaped to suit their purpose: horse shelter, tool shed, lofty carriage house where the grand old brougham is stored. I stopped to admire Henry's venerable John Deere, snug in its tractor-sized house, ready for the next day's field work. Past the home of my horse-loving neighbor, whose colt grew from sperm Fed-Exed across the country last year, I stopped again, this time to contemplate the thou-

sand shades of cream on the silo beside our hay barn, repository of a hundred bales and a dozen Angell bicycles. Then up the hill and through the gate to the ridge, where I strolled companionably with cows. Across the Hudson, the Catskills glowed blue in late-afternoon light and then pink as the sun began to set. On the way home, I visited my favorite bit of farm architecture: a barn door long ago painted teal, now weathered in ravishing patterns of blue and green and gray.

Seventy or eighty years from now, that door may be even more beautifully weathered. Or the door and the barn may have caved in by then or been flattened by the bulldozers that are creating suburban "estates" all over Dutchess County. "Things change over time," Henry says. I strive for his perspective, his equanimity, but mostly fail. Yesterday, as I headed

back toward our house, I thought again about a road trip I'd like to take next spring, at planting time in northeast Iowa. My hope is that Peter and I will fly to Chicago and drive west, cross the Mississippi at Dubuque, fifty miles south of Alvin Straight's bridge, then continue toward Waterloo on U.S. 20. Maybe we'll stop at Dyersville, to see the *Field of Dreams* baseball diamond. Maybe not. For sure, we'll drive dirt roads toward farms set back from the highway, to look close up at what I missed the first time around and take the measure of the changes wrought by time.

N° **69** / Nebraska 1993   N° **44** / Kansas 1993

N° 15 / Nebraska 1993

N° 8 / Colorado 1995

N° 41 / California 1995

N° 23 / California 1995

N° 1 / California 1995   **N° 2** / Kansas 1993

N° 25 / South Dakota 1993   **N° 49** / South Dakota 1993

N° **30** / Kansas 1993

N° **37** / California 1995

N° **28** / Montana 1993   N° **3** / South Dakota 1993

N° 7 / South Dakota 1993

N° 17 / California 1995

N° 66 / South Dakota 1993　　　　　　　　　　　　**N° 33** / South Dakota 1993

N° 40 / South Dakota 1993

N° 6 / Montana 1993

N° 50 / South Dakota 1993

N° 11 / South Dakota 1993

N° 9 / Missouri 1995

N° 22 / South Dakota 1993

PARTIALLY

5

PAINTED PICKUP TRUCKS

Trucks in Progress

Phil Patton

WHOLE CULTURES HAVE BEEN organized around totems that represent strength and skill, power as well as proficiency. For prehistoric peoples, these included the antelope and the caribou. Medieval Europe was ruled by the cult of the horse—"chivalry" comes from the root of *cheval*, the horse. Future historians may see in the detritus left by twenty-first-century America the signs of a culture built around the symbolism of the truck.

From the cartooned competitions of monster truck events, to the legendary pickup Sam Walton drove long after he became a billionaire, to Nashville's musical assertion that a truck is "a bed with wheels," the heaviest freight most trucks carry is symbolic. Trucks are rolling symbols of an idealized American past, heir to the Conestoga wagons that moved West, providing a sense of freedom, adventure, and escape—three qualities as deeply etched into the national con-

sciousness as those nineteenth-century wagon ruts that survive today on the Great Plains. But as the object of countless other cultural allusions, the truck rolls along in the collective unconscious perhaps as easily as it takes on the open road or trail. "Truck" has been made into a verb: to persevere, to travel steadily (nobody says "to car"). As rock and roll has its Rocket 88 and hot rod Lincoln, hip-hop its Escalades and Expedition sport utilities, the truck is the star vehicle of country music and Hollywood film.

The individual on the road, the professional nomad, is embodied in the containerized freight truck driver, or simply, "trucker." So even the Dodge Ram–driving suburbanite can feel a bit like Bogart at the wheel in *They Drive By Night*—the truck driver as hero. "America depends on trucks," the bumper stickers on the eighteen-wheelers proudly proclaim, avowing the trucker's role in a complex economy while still mythologizing him as the last cowboy.

EVER SINCE HENRY FORD'S Model T introduced a box on its back, allowing it to bear crops to town and store-bought goods back home, the truck has changed the American way of life. Only after World War II did Detroit bring styling elements from passenger cars to the humble truck, borrowing from the streamlined shapes of the age to soften the boxy edges. Today, pickup designers look to eighteen-wheelers. Dodge's Ram is styled after a giant Kenworth, while Ford and Chevy hark back to Mack. The recent SUV automotive trend stems from a small design revision; the sport utility vehicle stylizes the truck beneath a cabin, melding station wagon and truck. Women love SUVs more than men, the surveys show, seeing in them security and a high, upright prospect of the road.

But underneath, in all the promises of four-wheel drive and off-road capability, is a spiritual promise: that if things get too tough one can still leave the pavement and light out for the territory. "Trailblazer," "Pathfinder," "Explorer," and "Navigator" are all names for fancified trucks in a world where the trails have all been blazed and the paths paved. We drive them to keep our illusions alive.

THE POWER OF ANY MYTH increases the further it moves from its origins. So, naturally, the iconic power of the truck has increased the more distanced we become from our rural roots. Real trucks appeal for their utility and authenticity. They are tools, not toys. The beat-up truck was a product of necessity, not aesthetic choice—it was real life, not lifestyle. Notched and nicked with work, its metal and paint patches are the scars of honest labor, the primer-painted

replacement fender a badge of honor.

Trucks in process—hammered-out dents, primed, half-painted, or repainted—seem closer to buildings than vehicles. In their upright foursquare lines, trucks are never ashamed of wear. They proudly display the signs of additions and improvements, like houses. They, too, grow out of their environment, sharing the browns and greens of the landscape—colors straight from the American heartland. Their unpunctuated expanses of primer or enamel, with amped-up hue and tone, are like a rolling Rothko color-field painting or a freight-hauling Frankenthaler: abstract expressionism on wheels. They're readymades even Duchamp would be proud of. Without aiming for beauty, the truck achieves it nonetheless.

N° 11 / Memphis, Tennessee 1994

N° **23** / Lake Mead, Nevada 2000

N° 9 / Reno, Nevada 1993

N° 21 / Santa Barbara, California 2001

N° 62 / Oklahoma 2001

N° 6 / Ehrenburg, Arizona 2001

N° 42 / Havana, Alabama 1994

N° 20 / Van Horne, Texas 2001

N° 3 / Clermont, New York 2001

N° 5 / Central Indiana 1998

N° 19 / Death Valley, California 2001

N° 2 / Western New York 1998

N° 13 / Santa Barbara, California 2001

N° 14 / Montana 1999

N° 37 / Memphis, Tennessee 2001

N° 1 / Chester, West Virginia 2000

N° 15 / Eastern Kansas 2001

N° 35 / Cape Girardeau, Missouri 2001

N° 25 / West Texas 1999

N° **18** / Concord, California 1995

N° 51 / Arab, Missouri 2001

N° 52 / Kentucky 2001

N° 41 / Pennsylvania 2000

N° 10 / Sonestown, Pennsylvania 2001

N° 45 / Pennsylvania 2001

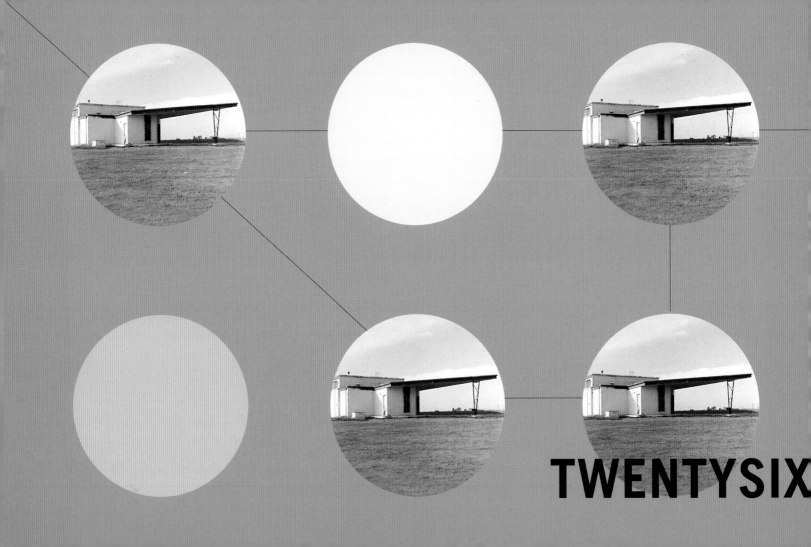

TWENTYSIX

6

ABANDONED GASOLINE STATIONS

Regarding Ruscha

Jeff Brouws

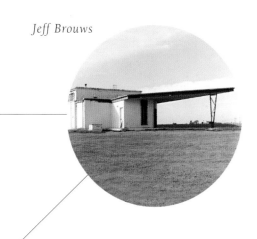

MAN-MADE FOREGROUNDS SHIFT, change, and get altered in our twenty-first-century world, but not the land forms behind them. Mountain ranges stay where they're put for thousands if not millions of years. Cultures fade, reemerge, and transform themselves (especially American culture!), but much of nature is immutable. These facts aided our search for Ed Ruscha's gas stations, for oftentimes only the background disclosed clues as to where one of them had been. K. and I had been stalking them since leaving California several days earlier. Plotting a course along Route 66 in December of 1991, from Barstow to Oklahoma City, we embarked on a re-photographic project with a rare first edition of Ed Ruscha's book *Twentysix Gasoline Stations* in hand—a book that I had swapped her father for earlier in the year. I was gleefully happy for the trade. *Twentysix Gasoline Stations*, decades out of print, had been a possession I long desired. Originally self-published by Ruscha in 1962, the book had twenty-six images of gasoline stations photographed on a road trip between Oklahoma City and Los Angeles. It would be the first of seventeen books that he would produce over the next fifteen years. Even with its low-tech, utilitarian look, it would go on to become possibly *the most* seminal influence on pop art, according to the critic Dave Hickey. I loved it for its unpretentious, straight-ahead quality. And naturally I loved it because I had always been enamored, since childhood, with gas stations.

I dig gas stations. My favorite was the Flying A just up the street from our two-story apartment on Oaklawn Avenue in Daly City, south of San Francisco. It faced Alemany Blvd., a busy four-lane thoroughfare bisecting the town, virtually guaranteeing that a steady flow of patrons would stop to gas up under the sweeping arch of its red and white canopy, which hung over the pumps like a cathedral honoring mobility. Prior to 7-11's or the modern convenience store, my mother routinely sent me to the station (because it was closer than the liquor store) with a hand-written note, giving me permission to buy Parliament cigarettes, her preferred brand, from the vending machine tucked inside the office. Amazingly, the graphics of the packaging mimicked the interior design of this small workspace, which reflected the sweeping angles of the station's roofline. This was, after all, 1964, with tail fins and curvilinear forms the fashion in advertising and architecture.

This gas station became my first true "hang out," a place to feel my coming manhood and be in the company of men who were good with their minds and hands. Interesting things occurred under the carhoods of America! I loved all the greasy tools, the polished steel of pneu-matic lifts, the smell of lubricants and gas fumes, and became visually intoxicated with the colorful STP, Pennzoil, Holly Carbs, Zoom, and Isky Cam stickers that were plastered everywhere. The Flying A emblem itself—a winged horse in flight (much like Mobil's Pegasus but depicted from the front instead of the side) also captured my absorbent imagination. It was there, too, that I smoked my first smoke and saw my first snatch (on a Snap-On Tools poster). It became sort of a semi-legal home-away-from-home. All in all, the station was my first introduction to graphic design, cigarettes, and immersion into a very masculine car-culture environment. This probably explains why I had to photograph them.

Returning to Ruscha: The first destination K. and I encountered was in Daggett, California. For some reason we never went looking for the two stations located in Los Angeles proper: I assumed there was too much ground to cover, too many possibilities, and not enough insight as to where Ruscha might have taken them. Maybe on Route 66 as it snaked through the LA basin—but maybe not. So I never tried. Anyway, back to Daggett: The station was no longer standing, it was an empty lot. We had to surmise what had once been there, since Ruscha's picture was a blurred night shot, with no distinguishing background geography to help reveal its former location. It was at a crossroads, a place where 66 made a hard right to tra-verse (and momentarily become) the town's main street. Logic dictated that a station would have been here. So I shot the vacant lot. One down, twenty-three to go.

Driving further along, the first easily recognizable one was the former Whiting Brothers station that Ruscha had placed near Ludlow (when in fact it was much closer to Newberry Springs, home to the fabled Bagdad Cafe that inspired the

131

movie of the same name). For some reason Ruscha had chosen to photograph this one from a distance, surrounding it with landscape. The service bays and office were converted to a residence, but the pumps still stood out front: red for regular, blue for supreme, white for mid-grade, all emblazoned with a "Hi-Desert Octane" logo. I detected no human presence. The highway itself rested in the winter sun with no traffic to call its own, as most of the cars and trucks now drove on I-40, a quarter mile to the north. We could have had a picnic in the middle of it, as we later would east of Shamrock, Texas.

Getting back in the car, we didn't hit our next station until we got to Needles, California. The familiar architecture of a Union 76 on the eastern edge of the city's business loop revealed itself to be Ruscha's next prey. Still in use, it was now an auto body shop with a tow truck out front. Operating in a semi-precise re-

photographic mode, I tried to match where Ruscha stood and the lens he used. This one was easy.

I've often wondered if the stations were chosen by Ed simply because he had to stop to gas up, or if there was a conceptual methodology behind his picture-making? Or was chance the defining criteria? The distance between the aforementioned towns of Daggett and Needles could easily represent a tankful of gas, but it doesn't account for why there are two stations from Winslow and Amarillo in *Twentysix*, unless of course he stopped at one on the way east, and then the other on the return trip west. A possibility. Through the little correspondence I did have with him, back in 1991, I know for a fact that he photographed other stations that he did not include in the book. Some art historians have also countered that Ruscha photographed thirteen stations going and thirteen coming, representing

the various Stations of the Cross. But methinks Ruscha had more secular intentions than spiritual ones.

So on our hunt went. The Flying A in Kingman had been torn down and the place was now a Best Western; the two in Williams seemed to have been demolished; the Phillips 66 in Flagstaff was easy to spot, an auto repair shop inhabited the building. We found the Bee Line in Holbrook, its unusual architecture still intact, but idle and no longer in use; and of course the long-operating Jackrabbit (THIS IS IT!) in Jackrabbit, Arizona, was still there, pumps a-pumping, though now a Mobil instead of a Texaco. One of my favorites in Ruscha's book, the Dixie station in Lupton, Arizona (with the Nash Rambler, hood raised, near the service island), was still extant, albeit now an empty shell of a building. The majestic butte behind it became the "tell" of the picture, helping us define the spot.

Among the best aspects of the search were the encounters we had with locals in trying to track down locations. If we initially had fears of over-handling the precious, rare art-object *Twentysix* had become for us (we were safely storing Ruscha's book in plastic sleeves and originally weren't intending to show it around), we inevitably gave up on that notion. In due course, crusty old mechanics, who someone "down the street" had referred us to, were bending back pages of *Twentysix* like it was a Clifton's repair manual, with greasy hands helping us crack the code, decipher the riddle— *to find these damn places!* The poor spine of the book, originally perfect-bound (a fragile type of binding to begin with), started looking desperately in need of chiropractic care. Instead of worrying about it, we let it go. The enthusiasm of the old-timers, giving us what information they could and delighting to be of service

to two photographers questing for the elusive, was payback enough. We were all in high spirits.

In time, with their help and on our own, we were able to capture many of the stations and luckily corralled all the Texas ones: Vega was now a tourist trap on Route 66; the one in Conway was now part of a chicken coop that we almost missed; the Fina in Groom was traceable by its unusual driveway. Still intact was the Mobil, minus the signage, in Shamrock, Texas. While I photographed many of these just for the sake of documenting what was, over three-quarters of them wouldn't be considered photogenic in their present condition or in a traditional sense, which explains why only one image made the cut for this *Readymades* selection (page 139). Unequivocally, it was the act of taking their portraits, from a historical perspective and for the connection to Ruscha, that fascinated me.

THE BEAUTY OF RUSCHA'S WORK is that it appears authorless, effortless, totally objective, artfully artless, which I think gives it a universal appeal, as if his voice and vision are ours, as if he's saying: *you could do this too.* His book *Twentysix Gasoline Stations* led me down the typological path; it made me want to photographically collect "types" of things as a way of systematically surveying the unique qualities of similar objects, a way to remind myself that everything in the world is interesting, mystifying, individual, and worthy of our attention, no matter how banal or ordinary.

133

N° 34 / Trona, California 1993

N° 44 / Santa Rosa, New Mexico 1996

N° 27 / Fall River, Kansas 1993

N° 52 / Boron, California 1993

N° 40 / Winnemucca, Nevada 1993

N° 55 / Shamrock, Texas 1991

N° 32 / Casper, Wyoming 1992

N° 49 / Mojave, California 1993

N° 41 / Lind, Washington 1992

N° 33 / Harlowton, Montana 1992

N° 37 / Mojave, California 1993

N° **29** / Formosa, California 1991

N° 28 / Little Lake, California 1992

N° 30 / Needles, California 1993

N° 42 / Salem, Oregon 1995

N° 46 / Santa Rosa, New Mexico 1996

N° 53 / Lind, Washington 1992

N° 36 / Texhoma, Oklahoma 1991

N° 48 / Nebraska 1993

N° 54 / Easton, Washington 1992

N° 45 / Midwest 1993

N° 31 / Groom, Texas 1991

N° 43 / Beaumont, California 1993

N° 62 / Green River, Wyoming 1993

N° 35 / Ritzville, Washington 1992

N° 38 / Calapatria, California 1993

7

FREIGHT CARS

Halfway Home

Joel Jensen

ONE HOBO'S DREAMS BEGIN HERE, and another's end. I'm standing in the dust-blown Las Vegas Union Pacific freight yard, a confluence of scattered rails nestled between I-15 and Glitter Gulch—Fremont Street. What I'm feeling has nothing to do with casino glamour, winnings or losings, and everything to do with a figurative roll of the dice and a train's direction. Riding freight trains can be a random, catch-as-catch-can experience. I'm heading home for Thanksgiving and hoping the odds are better than even that I'll catch-out before nightfall. I'm bound for glory or Iowa . . . whichever comes first.

Solitary musings linger in my head as a freight train rolls slowly across my field of vision. Boxcars, flat cars, grain cars, tankers, gondolas, and *auto carriers—auto carriers mind you(!)*—loaded with eastbound unlocked Toyota Celicas, keys in the ignition, tilt-back seats, woofers, and tweeters, enough gas for a test drive or two. I'm thinking *air-conditioned deserts, defrosted mountain passes. I won't freeze my ass off this time!* First-class Japanese accommodations all the way—not exactly "Seeing the USA in your Chevrolet"—but damn close. Some might think I'm cheating, killing purist notions of "high iron adventure"—that mode of travel reserved for contemporary, novice, recreational, weekend-wanderlust-boxcar-hopping "hobos," searching for fresh cocktail party banter. MasterCards in their wallets, wine and low-fat brie in their Eddie Bauer backpacks, business-class airline tickets for their return flight home. Me? All I've got is $20 tucked into a front jeans pocket, a pint of Jim Beam, and the clothes on my back. And I'm looking raggedy-assed to boot. Before I can even think of a return trip or what that might entail, I'll have to get to where I'm going first. I don't even own a valid credit card.

FREIGHT CAR CLACK AND CLANK reverberates, echoing off the canyons of skyscrapered casinos. I jump on an empty fifty-footer—a Southern Pacific Hydra-Cushion *especial*.

Thousand-mile paper litters the flooring; several dark figures emerge from the corners in the gathering gloom, like a welcoming committee. I'm on an adrenaline rush, backed with a bourbon chaser. Testing a smile, I advance cautiously in their midst, talking out loud, talking to no one. We're all alone even as we stand next to one another. I see imaginary fellow travelers— hobos from the old school. As the train rolls out into the desert, out past Meadow Valley Wash, we swap stories, recalling hard trips from yesteryear, the good ol' days. When I tell them that I jumped off a Rock Island boxcar "doin' thirty plus" they wince. They've been there, understand the hurt. Damn straight. I bitch about the train we hopped—a goddamn *dawg*—hobo-speak for short on power, long on freight. "We've lost our touch fellas, we'da never hopped a bitch like this, back when we was young and still had our teeth!" Laughing heartily, they nod in agreement, passing the bottle through a slow-moving desert mirage. Drifting into drink-induced sleep, I pity them, disap- pearing icons that they are. American Iconography. Trapped between nowhere and the hope of somewhere: terminal losers, or maybe just guys that decided not to participate in *the game*. Clutching a bottle tightly, I give thanks to Jesus. "I've got a notch or two up on them . . . huh, Lord?"

DRENCHED IN A FAMILIAR gritty sweat, I awaken to an unfamiliar place, train not moving, but heart and head pounding. Paranoia creeps in as freight car metal expands and contracts. Incessant wailing sounds, accompanied by a coyote's howl, mingle with the steady hiss of a leaky brake hose. White-knuckling a Toyota steering wheel, I'm trapped on a motionless train somewhere in Nevada or Utah, the land- scape foreboding and foreign. I've entered a zone of unknown. In my drunken delirium I imagine the Toyota plunging off the auto

163

carrier and shattering on the rails below. I'm thirsty, hungry, and cold. *Move* train *move! Please!*

A headlight in the distance grows larger, rapidly approaching, temporarily blinding me. Moonlight on stainless steel catches my eye, as late-night bar car faces are blurred in windows passing by. It's Amtrak's *Desert Wind* living up to its 79-mph expectations—here then gone, coming from Vegas. Somebody on that racehorse is headed back to Salt Lake City, poorer than me, wishing they'd done things differently—baccarat instead of blackjack, Church of the Latter Day Saints instead of Caesar's Palace. Contemplating life in first-class coach or in a freight car—not much difference. Regrets and remorse are companions to us all, always.

Slack rippling softly, and finally we're rollin' again. Praise Jesus. Leaving a side tracked place behind, heading for the main, we're closer to sunrise and somewhere, I think. Faster and faster, tripping on a freight car's mobile sense of place. Telephone poles rushing by, mile-a-minute hypnotics. Unpopulated desert "towns" represented by nothing more than black-lettered words on white moonlit sign-posts. No hobo campfires here. Nothing more than railroad labels, verifying west to east movement. I get located but still don't know where I am. Show me the lights of civilization—Milford, Delta, Interstate 80—anything alongside the Great Salt Lake. Offer me the opportunity to get off this fucking train and buy a side of hash browns and sausage, then lay my body in a Sally or rescue mission bed. "Hobo" huh? A "who-are-you-kidding" guilt comes between my conscience and the rolled-up windows of my Toyota freight car. Come on "hobo," the key's in the ignition, there's a quarter tank of gas

and climate control, surround yourself with warmth and a six-speaker sound

system. You want some light? You have a dashboard full of it: a cure-all for the encompassing darkness.

SOBER NOW AND COLD—a gentle rain falls as I wash my clothes in a pool of trackside water. A glance to the east reveals that rain in Odgen is snow in the Wasatch. There will be no sunrise today and freezing temperatures will prevail.

Five cars down the track a man and woman shuffle towards an open boxcar, the same one I'm heading for. Older and dirtier, plastic trash bags act as substitute raincoats covering their weariness. They've been at *this* game too long. Exchanging glances, we consider acknowledgment, then hesitate: meeting someone's eyes can be hard enough. Are they alcoholic transients or god-fearing Mormons? Or both? There's no way of knowing, and no manner in which to display my concern. Eastbound like Toyota and myself, they've chosen a freight train—a most economical means to an end. A momentary common denominator between us, like the hard, cold road we'll share for the next hours. Where is my Angel from Montgomery? We retire to our respective ends of the boxcar and I think sleep, and concentrate on primal urges for warmth and comfort: bedroll hibernation in a boxcar corner. Sleep will be a good thing, a necessary thing. Dreaming of yesterday's desert, trickles of Las Vegas sweat. Reminded of an old hobo's comment: "Hot, cold, hungry, thirsty. Always one or the other, or two or three out of four. If it's four out of four, you're probably dead or too drunk to know it!" Laughing out loud, train slack running through me—through us, always through us. Thoughts of hibernation and rest disappear as wheels begin to turn.

WAMSUTTER, WYOMING. Twelve A.M. Dancing to a train's rhythm . . . midnight at the ball. Back and forth, side to side, in and out. Partnered with someone who forgives the awkward steps, numbed like the feet and mind controlling them. A train is an unpredictable, rolling, uncompromising, and *very cold* entity—especially in November. Nobody's counting the cigarettes, as I light a new one off the last. I'll pass on the wine thank you, more Jim Beam for all of my friends. On the rocks, if you please.

Snow coalesces on the boxcar's floor, blown by high prairie winds through the wide-open door. Stand still and let it drift around your feet. The only insulation from the cold is a pocket around a hand—feeling pennies, wishing for quarters. Get off this fucking thing in Rawlins. Please. Eat some all-night food. Talk to a waitress, but don't tell her your story. We have a blizzard in common, that's enough. Maybe she'll be young and pretty, take a liking to me, invite me home and into her warm bed. She'd understand and admire the courage. Yeah, she would—nothing to feel sorry for here—probably lonelier than me. Your life sucks partner, but then again, so does everyone else's.

And I ain't even halfway home yet.

SOO 18900 / Montana 1999

D&H 24596 / New York 2000

PRR 4999132 / Ohio 1995

PC X29G / Ohio 1995

FGLK 182 / New York 1999

FGLK 181 / New York 1999

BN 217783 / California 2000

USLX 17041 / Pennsylvania 2000

NAHX 53044 / Montana 1999

USLX 14046 / Wyoming 1999

D&H 24659 / New York 1998

SOU 8978 / Western New York 1998

D&H 24505 / New York 2001

SOO 911185 / New York 2000

TSRD 30002 / *Pennsylvania 2000*

MEC 29214 / Maine 2001

D&H 001 / New York 2000

D&H 27085 / New York 2000

SLSF 600141 / Eastern Montana 1999

MEC "SCRAP" / Maine 2001

D&H 24500 / New York 1998

8

SIGNS

The
Annotated
City

Mark Frauenfelder

IN THE LATE 1990S I FREQUENTLY drove past the abandoned lot where Ship's Coffee Shop used to stand on La Cienega Boulevard in West Hollywood. The gigantic sign, mounted on a tall pole, was still there, resembling a rocket soaring over the street. About halfway down the pole was a smaller sign that read: NEVER CLOSES.

Whose cruel idea was it to leave that sign there? What kind of hollow-hearted person would allow it? But there it stood, years after Ship's had closed for good.

Designed in 1958, Ship's was a perfectly preserved model of Coffee Shop Modern architecture, also known as Googie (after a Los Angeles diner of the same name). It was a space-age, swooping, exuberantly positive style, which both reflected and stimulated society's unshakable optimism in modern technology.

Ship's exemplified a design esthetic that pointed the way to a future that was sure to arrive soon, a future in which we'd find ourselves heading to Ship's in flying cars to chow down on food that had been flash-baked in atomic-powered ovens. The atmosphere of the era crackled with invisible energy radiating from the jutting spires atop cafes and gas stations lining the roads. Parabolic arrows directed our attention to the fabulous fruits of postwar plenitude and pre-Sputnik superiority. It was a world in which jobs were abundant, leisure time was a birthright, and restaurants never closed.

But while we weren't paying attention, our dreams for a futuristic future eventually gave way to stucco-clad strip malls, horrendously boxy cars, and generic food packaging. Restaurants like Ship's became painful reminders of our failure to achieve a fusion-powered utopia, and one-by-one they starting dying. Ship's held out longer

than most. It was bulldozed in 1995 to make way for a truck rental company. The Ship's sign remains, and until recently, the smaller NEVER CLOSES sign stayed on the pole. In 2000, it too disappeared.

I miss the signs of the mid-twentieth century. How fun it must have been to drive down the main drag of any large town circa 1957. Hungry for dinner? Just look for a giant hamburger. Want to have some fun? Why, there's a thirty-foot-high bowling pin in the distance. Need to unwind? Head for the flying saucer–sized cocktail glass with the incandescent cherry in it.

The lights on these signs have burned out. Our world doesn't use signs like this anymore. Companies use bland, mass-produced logo-signs to advertise their brands. You won't find any behemoth percolators with steam puffing from the spout to tell you where to go for a cup of coffee. Instead, you've got the Starbucks mermaid (minus the nipples that graced its earlier incarnation) to let you know that wherever in the world you are, there will be no surprises—just a dose of care-fully metered conformity, approved by a consumer panel for mass market acceptability.

When a great building is destroyed, the sign is often the last thing to go. Like the label of an empty jar, an abandoned building's sign is a good indicator of the flavor, if not the actual taste, of what was once inside. Ironically, as a sign's once-bright, attention-grabbing paint begins to fade and peel, and the steel underneath acquires a patina of rust, it becomes more, not less, noticeable. Now that the arrows no longer point at anything they end up pointing to themselves, and back to us.

193

RANCH HOUSE CAFE / Vaughn, New Mexico 2000

BELL HOP / Bakersfield, California 1991

SANDMAN MOTEL / Reno, Nevada 1995

BELL HOP / Lordsburg, New Mexico 1996

BUS DEPOT / Anaconda, Montana 1999   **RIO PECOS TRUCK STOP** / Santa Rosa, New Mexico 2000

SHIP'S / Los Angeles, California 1996

CITY CLEANERS / Wayne, Nebraska 1993

COFFEE CUP / Wallace, Idaho 1993

FRESH CUP / Santa Cruz, California 1991

COFFEE CUP / Brawley, California 1989

COFFEE CUP / Winston-Salem, North Carolina 1990

ROCKET DRIVE-IN / Kingston, Idaho 1992

ROCKS-CAFE / Boron, California 1997

PARK (VERSO) / Gary, Indiana 2001

LONE STAR MOTEL / Pecos, Texas 1996

LAZO'S / Bakersfield, California 1996   **SUNBEAM** / Huron, South Dakota 1993

SOCIETY CLEANERS / Las Vegas, Nevada 1997

IDEAL CLEANERS / Bakersfield, California 1994

SAFE SALES / Cleveland, Ohio 1995

MASTER PADLOCKS / Cleveland, Ohio 1995

FRIES / Fresno, California 1995

PALM READER / Atwater, California 1989

SLOW SCHOOL ZONE / Amboy, California 1991

ARROW / Escabosa, New Mexico 2000

207

TOURIST HOME / Salem, Oregon 1993

9

TRAILERS

Marooned

Bruce Caron

THEY SIT IN THE BACK, out along the fence, under a tree. They stand immovable, silent. They wait long after waiting is an option. Once they were something: house and home, or vacation wagon. Now they are nothing to use and less to look at. These trailers are not actually abandoned, but they are marooned, lost without motion. Built for the road, they loiter gracelessly in backyards. Long after their logic of movement has been defeated, they simply exist.

Part of the problem is that such trailers are too big to trash, too heavy to haul, too old to sell, and too durable to melt voluntarily into the landscape. The cost of removing a twenty-four-foot-long, two-ton rectangle of aluminum and plywood from the backyard is something greater than one would care to imagine. Besides, they still have some use. And after the initial decade when the trailer fulfilled its active purpose and rode the freeways behind the family pickup, and after another decade when it became the spare bedroom for that less-than-welcome uncle, and after another decade when it housed the jumble of boxes of clothes and books and toys that might better have been tossed or given away except that there was "still room in the trailer," and then after yet more years when mice had found the vent space, and skunks nested in the storage bins, it stands there. Loaded to the ceiling, most likely, with the family's flotsam. And it is not alone. Look around, they are everywhere.

I dare you, reader, to travel any direction from anywhere in the U.S. for more than an hour without seeing an abandoned trailer. Even those of you who had, as I had, never noticed one. Innocence is once more defeated; I can no longer not see them. On my latest junket around Washington State I was first impressed, and then haunted by the spectacle of them—hulking aluminum boxes, wedged behind garages and barns. I began to wonder how very few of the hundreds of thousands of trailers built in the last seventy years had been destroyed (and what does it take to destroy a trailer?), and thus how many more were stacking up like giant rectangular isotopes with million-year half-lives: built to last, to say the least. And me, I'm a veteran of the backyard trailer corps. I should know better.

For many years a not-entirely abandoned trailer graced my own backyard. The sixteen-foot, 1968 Fireball was delivered to my backyard in 1985. For the next fifteen years it served serially as an art studio, a writer's den, and then a storage room. We had bought it to work in, not to travel with. By the late 1990s it still stood where it was first delivered. Over the years wisteria had embraced it, tendrils reaching into vents and louvered windows. Ferns crowded the wheel wells.

Inside, boxes of books and stacks of paintings were kept from the El Niño rains by its sturdy aluminum shell. But our plans to expand the rear deck required that the Fireball find a new home. After weeks of trimming and digging, the trailer looked not unlike it had in 1985. I removed the (original 1968!) tires to inspect the wheels. I replaced the wiring connections and reconnected the propane. But I could not guarantee that the undercarriage was still strong. I had no idea if this big aluminum box would ever be mobile again.

One Saturday, all it took was a large Jeep with a hitch on both the front and the back and some serious rubbernecking. The Fireball not only moved, it glided without event up the driveway and off with its new owner, who took it for a dollar and my gratitude, and who later installed a futon and velvet curtains and, I am told, tows it to dog shows in Fresno and Oxnard. Now it sits in her yard, where, in some years, it could again become immobile and finally abandoned. And be there, perhaps, forever. We may never know. Today, my own backyard is one of the few places where I can, with reliable comfort, not see an abandoned trailer. Amid the ephemera of the American roadside, trailers are its adamantine junk. The houses and the façades of roadside joints will weather to rot and dust some day and reveal what was always out in back. Another trailer.

211

N° 1 / Bombay Beach, California 1993

N° 23 / Bombay Beach, California 1993

N° **27** / Bombay Beach, California 1993

N° **33** / Keeler, California 1993

N° 6 / Bombay Beach, California 1993

N° 3 / Bombay Beach, California 1993

N° **13** / Bombay Beach, California 1993

N° 39 / Bombay Beach, California 1993   **N° 16** / Bombay Beach, California 1993

N° **34** / Bombay Beach, California 1993

N° **38** / Desert Shores, California 1993

N° 9 / Desert Shores, California 1993

N° 57 / Bombay Beach, California 1993

N° 21 / Eastern Pennsylvania 2001

N° **44** / Austerlitz, New York 2001

N° 29 / Bombay Beach, California 1993

N° 25 / Bombay Beach, California 1993

223

N° 7 / Keeler, California 1993

N° 19 / Altoona, Pennsylvania 2001

N° 14 / Bombay Beach, California 1993

N° 42 / Keeler, California 1993

N° 45 / Hoosick, New York 2001

N° 53 / Bombay Beach, California 1993   **N° 11** / Desert Shores, California 1993

N° 30 / Danby, Vermont 2001

10

BOWLING

Ten-Pin Tap

Wendy Burton

EVERY SUNDAY AFTERNOON when I was a child, my father would appropriate the tiny den off of our kitchen for what was billed as *Sports Watching Time*. He could have just as well called it *Serious Napping Time*, but to do so would have admitted to some kind of weary defeat. Because he was home infrequently from my seven-year-old point of view, I often chose to keep him company.

In the summer we would watch the Yankees beat the tar out of the Red Sox. I was hypnotized by the snail's pace of the game. The room would grow warm. My Dad would be stretched out on the couch and, as often as not, the sound of his snoring would drown out Mel Allen's voice. When this happened, my self-appointed task would be to turn the sound off on the television without waking my father up.

In the fall we would watch football. The massive size of the players fright-ened me, and my fear that they would paralyze each other at some point during the game greatly overshadowed the pleasure I might have taken in my tired father's sweet company.

The sport that was the pinnacle of Sunday Afternoon Spectating for me was Men's Pro Bowling. This was the sport of kings—average-looking men, who seemed nothing like professional athletes. Many, though not the *true* monarchs, looked decidedly out of shape, with bellies hanging over their belts, but my God could they ever bowl! Their grace astonished me. I learned to appreciate the beauty of a four-step delivery, with the right leg bent artfully behind the left. These men exhibited such precision and refinement as they launched their bowling balls with enormous power down the maple and pine lanes, crashing into the 10 pins and sending them airborne.

There were, of course, true kings of

the sport: Dick Weber, who was as lanky and handsome as he was skilled; Earl Anthony, the first man to win $1 million in tournament money—with his flattop haircut—was nicknamed Square Earl. He won forty-one separate titles on the Pro Bowling circuit. Watching these men bowl was to experience a miracle of hand-eye coordination—of subtle adjustments that would make the difference between a split and strike. And the earsplitting racket!! There was no way that either my father or I could fall asleep during a bowling match.

MY FATHER WAS A MUSIC PUBLISHER, and when I was twelve I recorded a Christmas song for Columbia Records. At this time of my life, bowling was one of the most acceptable outlets for boy-girl encounters. We would arrive at the alley in one of two ways: either descending en masse—large clusters of preteen girls and boys

perfecting the complicated ritual of flirtation while attempting to not throw an endless stream of gutter balls—or a few of the chosen would be chauffeured by parents, as a Couple, on a Preteen Date. This was something very special. I remember once sitting in the backseat of Larry Silverman's family Cadillac, Mrs. Silverman behind the wheel. The *Jim Lowe Show* was playing on the radio as we glided through the streets to the Walnut Lanes. My father had arranged with Mr. Lowe to play my record right at the hour that the Date was commencing. So we heard me sing on the radio. We arrived, Larry paid for my shoes, for my coke, and for my bowling. It was my own adolescent version of *Queen for a Day*.

LAST YEAR, AFTER WHAT WAS close to a thirty-year hiatus, I began to bowl again. I don't know what kept me away for so long. I love the rituals of bowling—not as a

spectator in front of a black-and-white television screen, but as a participant. It's so *wholesome*. My Dexter suede bowling shoes are very fetching. They are maroon and turquoise. I own my own bowling ball—a 12-pound matte blue ZONE that was supposed to improve my hook. It didn't. I don't have a hook shot. I throw a perfectly straight ball, which is fine with me. I'm learning to make it go where I point it. Sometimes.

One of the finest aspects of bowling is the mind-set that allows you to view each of the ten frames as a fresh start. You get two tries every frame, so even if you have the terrible misfortune of knocking down only a single pin with your first ball, you can rectify that with a well-placed second ball and score a spare. Learning to make spares seems to require more skill than throwing a strike. A strike ball obviously has to be well placed, with the ball most often hitting the 1–3 pocket, slamming

into the headpin. When this occurs, the ball takes down the 1, 3, 5, and 9 pins, and the other pins come crashing down, tumbled by deflected wood.

Spares demand that you learn to read the pins individually and know how they react in concert with one another. You have to have a strategy for varying pin configurations, and of course you have to actually be able to get the ball to go where you are aiming it. Sometimes, even though you *think* you've hit the pocket square on, you'll be left with either the 7 or the 10 pin standing belligerently in its corner. When this happens, you've been "tapped." Bowlers have developed their own lexicon of nicknames for spares. The 2-4-5-8 combination is known as "The Dinner Bucket." The 1-2-4-10 is called "The Washout." And the hair-yanking 7–10 split combination is called "The Bed Posts." "Double wood" is another dreaded phenomenon. It happens when one pin is left standing exactly in front of another. You have to hit the front pin head-on in order to knock down the cowardly one hiding behind it. This is not so easy to do.

I have experienced few joys as intense as bowling a string of strikes and spares. You have to not think about breaking the streak, or you'll lose your concentration and throw a gutter ball. But when you're in the zone, and you place that ball over and over again in the pocket—and the pins come slamming down in deafening disorder, well, there's almost nothing else like it. You forget about the kid eating hot dogs at the lane on the right, or the nine-step approach with the little jump-kick finish that the guy in the lane to your left keeps executing. You just zero in on the beauty of the ten pins and the feel of the ball as it leaves your hand, and you *know* you've thrown another ball straight and true, and it feels like you've

won the New York State lottery all by yourself.

Sometimes I bowl for the camaraderie. My husband occasionally drinks beer when he bowls, and seems to get better with each bottle. He is a powerful and graceful bowler, and I take pleasure in watching him. Sometimes, however, I like to bowl alone. I gradually work my way into it. If my first game is rotten, I simply move on to my second. I have been known to bowl five games in a row. My concentration improves as the afternoon wears on. Once I bowled a turkey (three consecutive strikes) in the tenth. It was the high point of my week. No, of my month! If I had to explain why, I don't know if I would be able. At the end of five games, my right arm aches, and that is immensely satisfying. I get to go home and sleep the righteous sleep of the weary. All I know is that I love to bowl. There is a purity to the sport and an intrinsic honesty to it.

It has a sweet and timeless innocence, and when I bowl, I feel somehow transported back to the fifties, to the *Donna Reed Show* and to keeping my father company on Sunday afternoons. I think if my father were alive today he would still be watching Men's Pro Bowling. I also think I might be able to persuade him to accompany me to the Ro-lin Lanes, to spot me a game or two.

235

N° 23 / California 1992   N° 57 / Midwest 1999

N° 21 / Wyoming 1993   **N° 19** / Oregon 1988

N° 8 / Ohio 2001　　　　　　　　　　　　　　　　N° 31 / Montana 1999

N° **6** / Illinois 2001

N° **15** / Kentucky 2001

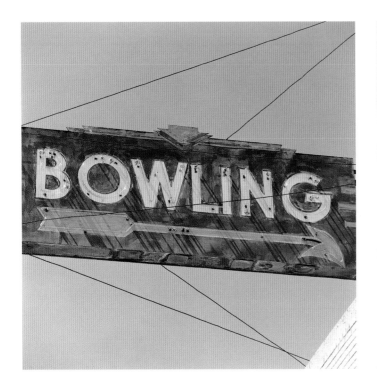

N° **17** / Montana 1999   N° **48** / Tennessee 2001

N° **16** / Kansas 1993

N° **11** / Missouri 1992

N° 40 / New York 1999

N° 25 / Idaho 1992

243

N° **9** / California 1989   N° **22** / Maine 2001

N° 24 / Wisconsin 1993   N° 35 / Utah 1997

N° **12** / Pennsylvania 2000

N° **4** / Nebraska 1999

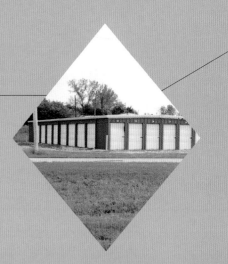

11

STORAGE UNITS

The Will to Box Up

Alan Rapp

I REMEMBER A BOOK I HAD as a kid, quaint in several ways. It was a *Ripley's Believe It or Not!* compendium, imparting factoids and pseudo-statistics in that uniquely blustering prose that read like fast-talking radio broadcasters sounded. Also, I bought it for fifty cents at an elderly couple's garage sale across the street; by the time it reached my hands it was already thirty years old.

In it I learned a number of remarkable things, among them that the entire world's population could fit in a container the volume of a cubic mile. And not only that, but the entire human population of the world throughout history, ever, would fit in there. Imagine that! The typically morose drawings that accompanied Ripley's mind-bending nuggets did not fail this time; a mountainous cube sat on a desolate patch of land, with gloomily rendered columns of people trudging toward it from a far horizon.

If this claim was ever true (is "true" the right word? I still imagine a hapless Ripley's staff accountant ended up doing those dubious equations), I knew it must have been impossible by the time I got wind of it in the early '80s. The world had grown by then, and surely everyone I could imagine—all the Brazilian and Chinese people, the Soviets and Australians—surely everyone couldn't fit in a mile-cube box. To suit the impossibly grim experiment by then, the world's populace would have had to find a bigger box.

Ripley's odd lesson in human population and volumetrics indicates that we compulsively put things in boxes, even our imaginary selves. It's this will to box up that helps explain the popularity of containers for the home, whether they're fancy hampers, fridgeware, "media storage," or milk crates. Often we cohabitate with our things in the boxes we call home. But when the things don't all fit, or if for some reason home is an uncertain box, we can put our things in another box, offsite. A 5' x 5' room is a good size for boxes and seasonal items, while 10' x 15' will accommodate three to four rooms' worth of furniture. Rental self-storage units are the last resort in a process that is meant to reflect home comfort; they are the military schools for our things that lack a place at home. The residents there are the surplus of individual accumulation, heirlooms too valuable or middling to discard.

Warehouses are traditionally where companies store their products and whole-sale goods. But now that individuals have their own individual warehouses in the form of self-storage, we are walking embodiments of capitalist destiny, realized on an individual basis. If a conceptual leap was made when capitalist concerns could incorporate—granting the entity the same legal status and rights as a per-son—in a sort of converse gesture the individual has now found footing with its corporate suzerain. When an individual has enough possessions to find the need to store them away from the nest in a storage unit, then the individual has fully capitalized, has achieved the corporate enterprise on a microscale.

This doesn't have to lend these units sinister undertones, however. Depending on how you look at it, this is an advance that could mark real sophistication with-in our society's economic structure. What can furnish the self-storage unit an air of menace is how it figures into schemes of evil, both real and imagined in pop culture. The mobile analog to the self-storage sheds are the rental trucks that constantly attend them, which have already written them-selves into the collective unconscious as faceless vehicles of terror. One-ton Ford

F350 Econoline vans and twenty-foot yellow trucks have new meaning for us now—not just in New York and Oklahoma City—but as a nation, and the meaning is purposeful destruction.

It is their anonymity and easy access that allow storage units to hide nastiness so well. Before the bombings of the 1990s, the popular movie adapted from Thomas Harris's *The Silence of the Lambs* explored this notion on a smaller scale. After the first meeting of Clarice Starling and Dr. Hannibal Lecter, he sends her on a quest for a murder victim whose body had never been found. "Look inside yourself," he tells her, and she shrewdly figures out the word game that leads her to a Your-Self Storage facility. The severed head she discovers there shows how depraved secrets can be hidden in these facilities, as long as you're paid through. But the evil is not as striking as the riddle of identity that Lecter proffers. Ensconced as they are in our society and unconscious, can these be zones that compel us to have a look within not only their musty holds, but also our very own selves?

Perhaps. The self-storage industry has conquered America, and now has its sights set on Europe. Whether they will succeed has yet to be seen. As with many other cultural innovations peculiar to America, the necessity was felt most only after they came into being. Now that we've learned to need them, we may also learn that they best belong in the environment they grew up in: a landscape of extended-stay corporate suites and other transitory architecture, traversed in rental cars and trucks.

N° 8 / Texas 2000

N° **7** / Illinois 2001

N° **14** / West Virginia 2001

N° 17 / Kentucky 2001

N° 20 / Texas 2001

N° **26** / Nebraska 2001

N° 15 / Pennsylvania 2001

N° 2 / Oklahoma 2001

N° 5 / Missouri 2001

N° 4 / Pennsylvania 2001

N° 19 / Arizona 2001

N° 35 / New York 2001

N° **12** / Tennessee 2001

N° **41** / Maine 2001

N° 25 / Pennsylvania 2001

About the Contributors

JEFF BROUWS is a photographer living in Red Hook, New York. A native Californian, he has criss-crossed America for the past 20 years in search of beauty among the mundane. His work can be found in various public and private collections including: the Whitney Museum of American Art, the J. Paul Getty Museum, the Cleveland Museum of Art and the Santa Barbara Museum of Art. Previous books include: *Highway: America's Endless Dream* and *Inside the Live Reptile Tent: The Twilight World of the Carnival Midway* (published by Chronicle Books).

WENDY BURTON is a photographer and literary agent. She lives in Red Hook, New York, with her husband, photographer Jeff Brouws.

BRUCE CARON is an urban cultural anthropologist and a documentary videographer. He is executive director of the New Media Studio, an independent, nonprofit, digital video and multimedia production studio in Santa Barbara, California, and president of the Federation for Earth Science Information Partners. He lives in Santa Barbara with his wife, Tinka.

MARK FRAUENFELDER is an illustrator and writer from Los Angeles. He, his wife, and four-year-old daughter are in the Studio City Islanders, a ukulele band specializing in hapa-haole songs from the 1920s.

DIANA GASTON is an independent curator and writer. Formerly the associate director of San Francisco Camerawork and curator at the Museum of Photographic Arts, she has curated numerous exhibitions of contemporary photography. Her exhibition catalogs include *Susan Rankaitis: Drawn* from *Science*; *Abelardo Morell and the Camera Eye*; and *Navigating by Light: Philipp Scholz Rittermann*. Her writing appears regularly in *Art On Paper*, *Artweek*, and *Art in America*.

JOEL JENSEN is a photographer living in Santa Barbara, California. He is a frequent contributor to *Trains* magazine and has had numerous freight train riding experiences across the American West.

M. MARK, a writer and editor who lives in Clinton Corners, New York, and in New York City, is working on a novel set in Manhattan, Kansas. She was founding editor of *VLS: The Village Voice Literary Supplement* and is currently editor of *PEN America: A Journal for Writers and Readers*. Mark has taught at Columbia University, NYU, and Bard College and currently teaches at Vassar College in Poughkeepsie, New York.

PHIL PATTON, one of America's most renowned journalists for design and popular culture, has written for the *New York Times*, the *Village Voice*, *Esquire*, *I.D.*, and *Art in America*. He is the author of *Open Road: A Celebration of the American Highway* and *Dreamland: Travels Inside the Secret World of Roswell and Area 51*.

ALAN RAPP is an editor and writer who lives in Oakland, California. His writing has appeared in *dwell*, *Wired*, *I.D.*, **Surface*, and other publications.

LUC SANTE is the author of *Low Life*, *Evidence*, and *The Factory of Facts*.

D. J. WALDIE is the author of *Holy Land: A Suburban Memoir* and the essays in *Real City: Downtown Los Angeles Inside/Out*. He is a frequent contributor to both the *Los Angeles Times* and the *New York Times*. He is a recipient of the Whiting Writers Award, the California Book Award, and National Endowment for the Arts and California Council for the Humanities fellowships. He is a member of the Los Angeles Institute for the Humanities. He is a city official in Lakewood, California, where he lives.

271

ACKNOWLEDGMENTS

Over the course of the last twenty years, as I honed my photographic skills, I was fortunate to receive friendship, support, and guidance from a wide array of people. It is only fitting that I take a moment here and express my gratitude.

In the gallery world I wish to acknowledge Craig and Karen Krull, and thank them for taking initial risks back in 1997, by giving a first-show to an unknown photographer; to Robert Mann, for taking a similar chance on the East Coast; to the wonderful staff of former and present employees at both galleries: Debra Bosniak, Ann Cain, Francesca Valerio, Lisa Granovsky, Devon Grosz, and Jennifer Tripp; to Robert Koch and Ada Takahashi for welcoming me in San Francisco. I'm indebted to each of you and humbled by, and grateful for, your enthusiasm and nurturance.

Over the years a group of collectors has graciously acquired my work, and I wish to thank them here: Bruce Berman, Burt Berman, Bill Brady, Tina and Bob Gale, Susan Grode, Jason Grode, Bill Levinson, Jonathan Novak, Rudi Reinfrank, and Michael Rubel. Your support and interest mean a great deal to me.

I also want to thank all of the talented writers who have contributed to this volume. I've long admired your work, read many of your books, and feel honored that your wordsmithing is such an integral part of *Readymades*. The words you've composed are insightful, intelligent, and elegant prose.

And to my editor, Alan Rapp, at Chronicle Books, I'm very appreciative of your persistent belief in my picture-making endeavors. Your vision and commitment keep the visual book world alive and vibrant. Thanks for being in my corner.

I'd also like to extend a heartfelt thanks to Erick Zanazanian of Erizan, mounter *extraordinaire,* in New York City; all the folks at NancyScans of Chatham, New York, who've selflessly guided me through the digital realm; and Marilyn Genter of Sterling Photography, Pleasant Valley, New York, for her excellent spotting and printing talents, not to mention her camaraderie and good cheer on the links. You all make the work flow so effortlessly and your technical prowess, craftsmanship, and pursuit of exceellence is impressive. Every photographer should be so lucky.

On top of this, a group of friends has shown unwavering encouragement every step of the way.

Many have also accompanied me on photographic expeditions or been an inspiration with their own photography, painting, or sculpture—all have enriched my life. Blessings to Nell Campbell, Ginny Brush, Matt Ingersoll, Kim Kavish, Cathy Maybury, Wayne Depperman, Ed Delvers, Richard Steinheimer, Jerry Burchman, Maria Marewski, Robert Beckmann, Trey Rainey, and Ed Gregory.

Last, but certainly not least, my wonderful wife, Wendy, has been there unfailingly. Not only did she act as project manager for *Readymades*, she's its creative director and codesigner. Her artist's insight and valued opinions appear throughout. Thank you, sweetheart.

Jeff Brouws
Red Hook, New York